What Men Want

The 10 Irresistible Traits
High-Quality Men Want
In A Woman

Ray Lemon

Contents

INTRODUCTION

A very small portion of our female population understands what men truly want when choosing a partner for a long-term relationship. This is primarily due the inaccurate information that the media spreads on a daily basis. The media employs smart marketing tactics to impose its agenda on the world; thus, confusing most women as to what men really want in them. Obviously the purpose for doing this is financial gain.

The media primarily survives on advertisement; therefore, they are willing to do and say anything in order to sell the latest products. They frequently try to associate their products with a major problem or desire that women have, and it often happens to be finding a quality guy to start a serious relationship with and get married. For these companies, spending millions of dollars on a world-class marketing team makes perfect sense because they know that this team will find a perfect way to make their target audience believe that they must buy one of their products in order to appear attractive to men. In other words, they aim to make you believe that attraction is primarily physical. This helps them promote all kinds of products and make a lot of money in the process.

When a marketing team goes to work trying to create the perfect campaign that will sell a company's product, they keep in mind that one of the greater weaknesses in today's society is that fewer and fewer families are doing their jobs to educate young women on what makes them truly desirable to high-quality men. If you look at what the media teaches women today, you can clearly see a message that states, all you need is a certain look in order to attract a great man. As you have probably guessed, this is what helps these huge companies sell things like expensive clothing, cosmetics, diet pill and programs, etc.

While it's true that looks matter to a certain

extent, what they don't tell you is that men look very differently at women when it comes to building a committed relationship versus just finding a girl to have fun with. As a result, what ends up happening repeatedly is that women get used and treated like dirt by low-quality men, which leaves many of them wondering why they can never attract a man who will truly value their inner qualities. Make no mistake, this is a huge problem for all types women regardless of how they look.

I know that deep down you realize that looks aren't the only thing that matter when it comes to dating and relationships. In fact, you are probably very aware of what's going on and much more intelligent than the type of women that I have described up to this point. However, do you know the specific characteristics that quality men desire in women that they would want to get serious with? If you do, then this book is probably not going to be very helpful to you. On the other hand, if you don't know the characteristics a man wants to see in you that will help him decide whether you are the right woman for him, then you need to read this book.

By providing these ten qualities my goal is to

show you that the way you look isn't necessarily the most important thing when it comes to attracting a quality man. There are far more things beyond your physical appearance that are extremely important to good masculine men. Does your physical appearance play a role in your dating life? Yes, of course it does. However, as you will see later in this book, your looks can also be a hindrance if they are not combined with these ten qualities that great men truly desire in women. Even though this may be hard to believe, I want you to know that if you are not the best looking woman in the world you may actually have an upper hand over a gorgeous woman if you possess these ten qualities. Read further and find out why.

As you read this book, I want you to pay attention and try to notice one underlying factor that serves as the foundations for all ten of these desirable qualities. I will reveal what this foundation is at the end of the book. Just by developing this one characteristic in yourself, all kinds of quality men will begin to see you as a woman they would love to be in a committed relationship with.

Chapter One

Physical Qualities

Women often assume that men are only interested in one thing; how soon they will get to have sex with them. It's actually a little more complicated than that. Although physical attributes are what attract a man to a woman, it's not all about being shaped like a figure eight in order to grab a guy's attention. I want this chapter to help you understand that men are interested in much more than just your looks when they search for a member of the opposite sex. This is good news because you have limited control over how you look.

There is no need to think that if you're not a shapely blonde that you have no hope of getting a date. The reality is that women who are considered average looking regularly find great guys and have fulfilling relationships.

How Attractive Do You Really Needs To Be?

Well, there's no doubt that a woman who is considered beautiful will turn a man's head, that's only natural. But in our society, the media tries to convince you that designer clothes, shoes, and makeup are required in order to catch a man. It's actually not that serious for the average guy.

The men who are after extremely beautiful women are usually immature and always chase what they consider to be a better deal. These guys typically don't have much success with women, let alone beautiful ones. For these immature men, attaining a relationship with a woman who they consider a trophy is a way to boost their status with others. They look to impress family, colleagues and friends just to prove to them that they are successful. This is simply a technique that helps mask their lack of self-esteem.

Men who tend to be more successful with women understand that a pretty face isn't everything. They have been involved with gorgeous women and therefore realize that they are no more special than average looking women. Once a man gets over trying to pursue beautiful women exclusively, he starts seeing the other wonderful attributes that women possess.

What we find attractive is totally subjective. Therefore, it's important to note that what is considered attractive is going to be different among men. Some guys like short women, others like tall; some like blondes, or prefer brunettes or redheads; some are into curvy women, others like women that are slim; some guys like small breasts, other prefer larger ones... and the list goes on.

So regardless of your body type and what you look like, there will be men that are attracted to you and some that won't be interested at all. That goes for women who are considered very beautiful, too! But as you read further, you will see that even if you don't fit in the exact category of a man's physical preference of women he's normally attracted to, that doesn't mean he won't be interested in you.

The Real Reason Why Even Secure Men Go For Pretty Girls

Since a man really doesn't know what a woman is like until after he gets to know her, if given a choice, he'll go for the prettiest woman in the room. He doesn't know anything about her yet so he'll want to find out more and see if there's a connection, which if you think about it is logical. Also, just because the woman is beautiful doesn't mean that the man is interested in a long-term relationship with her. This just may be the one night stand he's looking for.

A more beautiful woman also tends to have an air of confidence about her. She's had her ego boosted by many different people on a daily basis. This energy is something men find attractive. Pay attention, confidence is sexy! This is something we will cover in depth in a later chapter.

You may be thinking about how to get a man's attention after this explanation, since it's obvious they're most likely to approach a more attractive woman first. What you need to realize is that men who are looking for women in places like clubs and bars are usually looking for very short-term encounters. This is not where you want to seek out potential boyfriends or husbands anyway. If you intend to find a partner who will value your inner qualities as much as your physical qualities your chances improve drastically if you look for them elsewhere.

Even though a woman's appearance is not the most important thing to a man, do not think that you shouldn't care about the way you look. You do not have to be the best looking woman on the planet, but a guy won't approach you if he thinks you're extremely unattractive.

The goal is to be the best you that you can be. It's important to put some effort into looking your best without overdoing it. When I say without overdoing it, I mean that you should avoid applying excessive amount of makeup or going to the extreme like having cosmetic surgery. This way, men can check off looks on their list as satisfactory and move on to see what other qualities you have.

If you are not extremely attractive you

actually have more options available to you in terms of men to date. That's because most men tend to be intimidated by very beautiful women. Even though they are always looking them over and imagining being with them, they usually don't have the courage to approach them and ask them out. This type of attention doesn't mean anything to an attractive woman since it won't get her a man who is interested in pursuing a relationship with her for the right reasons.

What Men Generally Find Attractive In Women

We can now discuss what men tend to like as far as physical attributes in women. As mentioned earlier, men's preferences will vary, but this is a general outline of what guys tend to find appealing.

Figure:

As far as physique goes, most guys prefer curvy women over very thin women. The supermodels on the catwalk that are super thin are not that attractive to the average man. Although the media would often have you believe otherwise, most men would prefer you to be slightly overweight than underweight. Also, don't obsess about your butt. Most men don't mind a little extra in that area.

This doesn't mean that you shouldn't take care of yourself and keep in good shape. The most important part of your figure is being healthy and feeling good about yourself. Remember what I said earlier about confidence, it really boosts a woman's sex appeal!

Hair:

Most men are open about hair color but the majority of us do have a preference for longer hair. It tends to give a woman a more youthful look. There is a tendency for women to cut their hair after they reach their 30's and settle down with children. But it doesn't really work that well for attracting men, and unless it is a particularly attractive cut, it can look masculine. Of course long hair doesn't work for every woman, so remember to work with what you have and go by what looks best on you.

Breasts:

There's a lot of attention from the media

coverage in our society regarding women's breasts. Often the media tries to make you believe that large breasts are most attractive but the truth is that men have different preferences in this area as well. In fact, men tend to have long term relationships with women who have average sized breast the most. Most guys want big enough that they distinguish her as being a female but not so large that she draws attention to herself and people are wondering if they are real. The size of your breasts overall will not determine your attractiveness to men unless you are self-conscious about your body. The type of man you would consider being in a relationship with is looking at the total package, not just your chest.

Height:

A woman's height is the one attribute men usually have no preference in. But one important point to note is that some men feel uncomfortable with women who are taller than they are. This is not really a problem for most women because even if they are tall they can always find men who are their height or taller.

Clothing:

What a woman wears is not of great importance to most men. You don't have to come up with expensive designer outfits in order to be attractive. Clothing that fits well and accentuates your attributes, but doesn't flaunt them work well. In other words, dress comfortably in well fitting clothes.

Wearing clothing that is considered very sexy will get you a lot of attention from men, but they won't be thinking about getting involved in a relationship. They will only be wondering how fast they can get you into bed. Skirts should be close to knee length and not too much cleavage should be revealed. He needs to be able to see you as a girlfriend or wife, not a hooker! One simple trick to make sure that what you are wearing will send the right message is to ask yourself if you would feel comfortable meeting his parents while wearing that outfit.

Cosmetics:

With makeup, less really is more. Some makeup is fine but the goal is to have a natural look, which is what most men prefer. Also, when a woman is pouring makeup on really thick a guy starts wondering what she has to hide and what she will look like in the morning.

Men aren't expecting you to be perfect, and a woman who is trying too hard to cover a couple of laugh lines or a small acne scar says that she doesn't like herself very much. Everyone has some imperfections of this type, so live with it. Also, people pick up cues from how you treat yourself. They feel that how you treat yourself is how they should treat you as well. If you like yourself and are comfortable with who you are, other people will like you too. Men are looking for self-confident women to establish relationships with, not ones who are insecure.

Chapter Two

Self-Esteem

As I have mentioned in the previous chapter, outer beauty only serves to attract some men initially, but it isn't enough to keep them interested for the long term. Beauty is a subjective word that manifests itself in many different ways. Your level of self-esteem is what influences thoughts, actions, and how you come across to others. How you view yourself shows in many aspects of your being. Men who are emotionally stable and fit for high-quality relationships have a moderate to high level of self-esteem, and will be looking for the same in a partner.

What Is Self-Esteem?

Self-esteem is the degree to which you like yourself and are comfortable with who you are. It is believing that you are a worthwhile individual with a lot to offer yourself and others. When your self-esteem is high, you believe in your abilities. You hold your head high because there is no reason to lower it. When you make mistakes you realize that you're human, and try to correct them. If you possess physical attributes that some may consider to be unattractive, that is their opinion and not yours. Your beauty is found within the way to live your life in line with your true values. You respect yourself and will not easily allow others to show you disrespect.

If your self-esteem is low, you have a lack of self-respect and you undervalue yourself. You will tend to have a negative outlook and expect the same treatment from others. You tend to dwell on the aspects of yourself that you don't like and it often shows in your thoughts, actions and interactions with other people. There is also a tendency to treat others the same way you treat yourself. This can seriously get in the way of forming a healthy loving relationship with a potential partner.

Positives And Negatives Attract More Of The Same

Low self-esteem creates a persona that doesn't let the beauty of the real you shine. The negative habits that are telltale signs of this condition are a real turn off to well-adjusted men who are looking for a compatible mate. You may well attract men, but they will usually have the same type of issues, or be looking for a partner that they can dominate, and not treat as an equal. Women who have a positive attitude about themselves tend to like who they are, and know what they want out of life. Knowing and liking yourself inside and out will help you avoid settling for a relationship that is unbalanced. The same is true for men. If you want to attract a well-balanced man that is interested in a healthy and happy relationship, then building your self-esteem is the best place to start.

What Healthy Stable Men Are Looking For In Women

Men can tell at a glance, or when first meeting with a woman, how much she truly values herself. When you like yourself, it shows in how you look, and the energy that you send out. It shows in your mannerisms, the way you talk, and the general attitude you project. Men are looking for someone who is enjoyable to be around. Well-adjusted men are most attracted to a woman who can be herself, laugh easily and not repress her personality out of fear of being rejected. Who wants to be around someone who constantly brings them down? The answer is, a person who is not well-adjusted themselves, and thrives on negative interactions. In general, men try to avoid women who are going to bring them down.

Signs Of Low Self-Esteem

Most excessive behaviors that swing from attention-getting to avoidance are signs of self-esteem issues. Some signs that are a dead give away are extremes in self-absorption, constantly fishing for compliments, obnoxious behaviors or exaggerating situations to get attention. Creating drama where none would otherwise exist is common, and it's something that men avoid with a passion.

Some women belittle others to try to elevate

themselves. Others give in to the demands of others even if it goes against their wishes. They feel that they are not worthy of respect. They do not respect themselves, nor do they require others to respect them. Any type of overcompensation, such as being excessively loud, seeking to be the center of attention, wearing tons of makeup or clothing that is distracting to others can be signals that self-esteem is at a low ebb.

A Little Balance Goes A Long Way

We all do zany things at one time or another, and it makes life more interesting. Finding a balance so you're not all over the map is important when you want to attract a well-balanced man. Stability and reliability are qualities that are highly prized by men. They tend to steer away from women who are highly unpredictable or who tend to stir up drama. The best way to get a man's attention is to let your true inner beauty shine and be the best you that you can be. This means pleasing yourself first. When you are happy with yourself, you'll project the energy automatically and other people will feel it. It's one of the most powerful attractants in the world. This doesn't mean that you should aim to become arrogant or self-centered. What it does mean is achieving a balance that is somewhere in the middle.

How To End The Cycle Of Behaviors That Indicate Low Self-Esteem

This begins with you coming to the realization that you have the potential, regardless of your level of physical attractiveness, to possess qualities that are attractive both to men, and to yourself. The hard work starts with learning to like and love yourself. You can change some of your outward behaviors and fake it if you like, but the underlying problem will only resurface in other ways. Find your inner beauty and start giving yourself the credit that you deserve.

If there is something you legitimately don't like about yourself, change it. Forgive mistakes you've made and move on. Don't dwell on the past but use it as a stepping stone to create a better future. Stop saying negative things about yourself to others. Make notes about the general comments you make during an average day. Ask yourself how you can adjust your attitude to reflect a more positive estimation of your own value. Your words will be an overall reflection of your self-esteem and monitoring this will help you to make changes as you go. It's hard work and takes a little time to change burned in beliefs and habits, but it is highly doable and you can change your life by taking charge of this.

One of the most important things that make a woman attractive to well-adjusted men is her self-esteem. This is the driver that controls how you come across to men because it affects your attitudes and actions. People come to know one another by the inner energy that they project to the outside. When self-esteem is high and balanced, the genuine you is not hiding behind a fence of negative self-perceptions and beliefs. You become more available to others, and in turn, more attractive to men looking for a wonderful lady who is capable of inspiring the development of that special feeling. Love, respect and acceptance. It goes a long way and it's a two way street.

Chapter Three

Confidence

The way a woman carries herself and presents who she is shows in her overall appearance. It is also discernible through the energy that she projects from within. This goes far beyond the clothing and makeup that she may be wearing. The aura of confidence is fairly easy to pick up on. Men who have self-confidence and are seeking a compatible potential partner will be more strongly attracted to a woman who is confident in herself.

What Is Confidence?

Confidence is an energy that emanates from the core of your being and tells others who you are. When you are confident, you have a high level of self-esteem, which includes believing in your abilities, liking and respecting yourself for who you are, and making no apologies for your own uniqueness as an individual. You are comfortable in your own skin so to speak, and feel no awkwardness in being yourself for fear of judgment from others. Confidence is also the lack of self-doubt, little or no need for outside validation as a person, and the absence of an overwhelming fear of rejection. We all have moments of self-doubt, but for the confident person, this is short lived. For those with a lack of confidence, it can become a way of life.

Signs of A Lack of Confidence

Women who lack confidence generally have low self-esteem as well. The two go hand in hand. When a woman doesn't like herself it shows in most aspects of her life. There is a tendency to project a negative outlook on life in general, which is drawn from her self-image. Instead of allowing her true beauty and personality to show through, it is usually veiled behind a host of defenses that offer protection from the perceived threats of the world outside. The fear of rejection and failure is a dominant trait. This is felt in the energy that she projects from within. When trying to establish a romantic relationship there is often drama caused by her need for reassurance and issues of mistrust.

The Reasons Why Men Are Attracted To Women With Confidence

Most men are able to easily pick up on the subtle vibes that women send out. Women with confidence are easier to get to know than those without. There are no contrived barricades in the way and her true personality is available for viewing. There is no need for games such as playing hard to get, fishing for compliments, or constantly needing assurance of her worth. This is because she knows her value and has a firm respect for herself that doesn't require the confirmation of someone else.

The main reason that confidence is an attractive trait for men is that it signals the increased likelihood of a stable and enjoyable relationship. A confident woman brings as much to a relationship as she takes from it and less friction is apt to be the result. Men do not enjoy playing emotional games that will demand their attention from a woman who is constantly in turmoil and crisis. It can be exhausting and frustrating. Straightforward interactions leave more time for enjoying life and attending to more important details of the relationship, such as getting to know each other better.

Confident women know who they are and where they're going in life. They own their personalities and are aware of their own abilities complete with amazing talents and flaws. They have a reasonable and balanced opinion of themselves that doesn't swing from one extreme to the other. With this type of positive outlook, a woman has much more to offer a man in a relationship. The elements of confidence combine to form better partnerships in which each is pulling their fair share of the weight.

How To Build Confidence

Confidence is built by getting to know yourself including your talents, abilities, flaws and unique personality type. First of all, start owning the entire package. Don't blame your misery on other people because you are the only one who is responsible for your thoughts, actions and attitudes. Believe me, with a little work, these are all things that can evolve into a more positive set of processes.

Acceptance of the entire package of who you are is the next vital step. If there are things you don't like about yourself and they are reasonably changeable, then start working on them. This will give you another reason to take pride in your accomplishments versus self-criticism. Focus on the positive aspects of who you are and start sharing the love.

When you learn to love, like, respect and honor yourself it will begin to show in every area of your life. Your speech patterns will change from self-bashing themes to more positive affirmations of what's going on in your life. You will feel less need for reassurance from others and in time your focus will be less on yourself and more upon the interests that you develop. All of these steps will help in establishing the firm belief that you are a worthwhile and valuable person, without the need for outside confirmation.

Confidence is one of the most attractive qualities in women that men pick up on almost immediately. It signals that she is a whole person that is capable of establishing a meaningful and mutual relationship. First impressions are generally lasting ones and the energy that confidence generates sets a positive tone that makes men have a stronger desire to investigate further. With less emotional turmoil and baggage to sift through, life is more enjoyable and less stressful. It's not much fun to spend half of the time you're with someone trying to sort out their personal issues that are generally self-inflicted.

Men who have had experience with different personality types in relationships are particularly keen in discerning the signals that women send out. They have learned how certain behaviors can signal the start of a lovely relationship, or the beginning of a potential nightmare. Confident and savvy men are most attracted to confident women who are capable of forming a mutual and emotionally healthy relationship.

Chapter Four

Emotions

There have been many discussions among women about what attracts a man and keeps him interested. The same can be said of men who are tired of feeling the effects of a woman who is never happy, and hoping for some advice. One of the most important qualities that a woman can possess is an abundance of positive emotions and a joyful nature. Combine this with a healthy balance of intelligence and common sense and you have a winning combination. These are some of the most highly prized traits that men look for in women. This indicates that she is content with herself, confident and happy with life. The opposite can be said of a woman who scowls and complains the majority of the time.

How Men Respond To Positive Emotions

When a woman projects positive emotions, it surrounds her with an aura of pleasantness. She is fun to be around and willing to share her joy by uplifting her partner. Men enjoy the security of knowing that after a hard day's work, they can escape the stress of the workplace by coming home to a positive environment where they are appreciated and shown consideration.

A joyful woman seeks to share the good in her life and this translates into doing both small and big things that make a man feel good about himself. She compliments him for accomplishments and loves him for who he is and not necessarily what he can do for her. In short, she gives him a reason to want to come home, or to be with her because she improves the quality of his life in many different ways. When a woman is positive, a man feels like he is pleasing her and feels more free to be himself. It's much easier to have an open and honest relationship when communication is positive and productive.

The Effect Of Negativity On Men

Women who are unhappy tend to have a plethora of negative emotions. This generally comes out in her body language, her attitude and the things that she says. Constant complaining or talking about personal problems creates anxiety in men and is often perceived as a deluge of negativity, similar to drowning in a river of misery. This is particularly true when the negativity is aimed directly at him. Instead of a refuge from life's frequent difficulties, his time spent with her can become an excursion into criticism and put-downs. Nobody needs that in their lives and this is one of the reasons why negative emotions in women are a real turn off for men.

Specific Effects Of Drama On Men

Drama and crisis are man killers. When a man has to come home to the unknown, the result is dread and chaos in his mind. There's nothing more draining than coming home from work to face a new crisis or to be confronted with a list of complaints or accusations. Most often, women who thrive on drama create impossible situations with no remedy. This can make a man feel trapped in a situation in which there is no solution. These behaviors amount to an emotional whipping and are a form of emotional battery. When you compare this scenario with the case of a guy who is looking forward to the nurturing love and comfort his woman brings him, it's no contest. Men prefer women who take a positive and joyful approach to life.

Joy Tempered With Maturity

It's great to be able to share jokes and laughter with a woman, but too much of a good thing can become irritating. A woman who is continually laughing, or cracking jokes, particularly of the less appropriate nature, can get outworn fast. It can also give the impression that the woman is silly and immature. A woman who shows her intelligence and maturity while exhibiting positive emotions is more fun to be around. An occasional zany outburst can be entertaining and fun, but moderation is the key to keeping a man interested.

The Importance Of Achieving A Healthy Balance Of Emotions

A woman who acts happy all of the time can be perceived as being phony. Joyfulness is a state of contentment and being thankful, and this is a very positive thing. But there are times when it is appropriate to tone it down and go with the flow. Showing emotions appropriate for the situation is also important. You can still have a positive attitude even when times call for a more laid back approach.

How To Become More Joyful And Positive

If you have a tendency to feel negative it probably shows in your thoughts, actions, and interactions with others. This can cause men with positive emotions to run the other way. But all is not lost. There are ways that you can turn this around and become a more positive person. Regardless of the circumstances which may have caused you pain, anger or unhappiness in your life, you can begin the healing process and claim the joyfulness that each of us deserves.

First of all, learn to accept that nobody is perfect. This includes anyone that has caused you pain, and even you yourself. Find ways to let go of anger, resentment and any other negative emotions that are holding you back. Next, learn to love, like and accept yourself for exactly who you are right now. Focus upon all of the positive things in your life. If changes need to be made, then make them. As you change on the inside, you'll notice that your outward behaviors will follow suit.

Men are more strongly attracted to women who show positive emotions and joyfulness. These are qualities that indicate the possibility of a healthier relationship that will be uplifting and more pleasurable. Men know that women with negative attitudes are more likely to bring them down on an emotional level, and create an unhappy environment. Women with negative attitudes may well attract men with similar emotions, which can create a rocky experience. This is why it's so important for women to maintain a well-balanced attitude of positive joyfulness.

Chapter Five

Femininity

As we have already established, well-adjusted men are looking for women with a positive mental attitude, aside from physical attractiveness. However, it doesn't stop there because femininity is another important quality that most men want in a long-term relationship.

What Is Femininity?

Basically, femininity is the energy associated with female behavior. This energy can be detected by any person who is surrounded by women, just as much as masculinity can be detected when surrounded by men. Most people tend to have both characteristics because they are each needed to function efficiently in our daily lives; however, women tend to be more feminine and men more masculine.

It is important to keep these energies in balance because as far as attraction to the opposite sex goes, women tend to be interested in men who act more masculine, while men are usually drawn to women who act more feminine.

In our society, the main message that women tend to receive is that men are looking for them to be extremely physically attractive, but the truth is that what we really want is for women to be more feminine. Even though physical attraction is one aspect of femininity, it also has a lot to do with a woman's inner qualities. As I have mentioned earlier, a man who seeks out a woman strictly for her beauty tends to be insecure and is usually looking for approval from others. This type of man doesn't usually take time to consider whether this woman will appreciate him and add to his quality of life.

I should also mention that weakness is not considered feminine or attractive. Well-adjusted men are looking for women who can be their equal while at the same time secure enough to allow them to lead. A strong woman knows that she doesn't have to prove anything to anyone and is comfortable allowing the man to make decisions for both of them. For instance, a woman should be comfortable with having a man choose the restaurant they go to.

Many women appear insecure because their beliefs make them feel that allowing a man to lead will diminish their independence. They carry an attitude that says they don't need anyone and can do everything themselves. This is a huge turn off for men because they feel like they will never be able to satisfy her, or be the man in the relationship.

How It Impacts Your Dating Life

Femininity has more to do with being as opposed to achieving goals. The actions involved are about being supportive and allowing the man to lead. You may notice that men are not really interested in finding out about your goals in life initially unless they see how it can help them reach their own.

This is also why women who come across as goal oriented in the beginning of the relationship, such as having a time table to get married, come off as pushy. It's not that a woman shouldn't expect anything from a man; she should, but no guy wants to feel like the only reason you're with him is to get what you want. He wants to feel genuine love and to be admired for who he is.

In a relationship, a woman needs to trust that if she gives her gift of femininity to a mature man, he will reciprocate and give her the gift of masculinity in return. This way everyone gets what they need. Although a man may be very successful in his business and financial life, without a woman that can provide the gift of feminine energy he will almost always end up feel lonely and unsuccessful.

How To Use Your Femininity In Dating and Relationships

In order for a man to be attracted to you beyond something physical in the early stages of your relationship you must be willing to open your feminine side to him. In other words, let him take the lead. Let him be the first one to make contact, to ask you out and make plans. He should be in charge of organizing and planning things that you will do together and of course proposing to you, if the relationship develops to that stage.

Don't nag, give unsolicited advice, or come up with ideas and run with them on your own. Also, definitely do not criticize him on his efforts. Once he gets to know you better he will value your opinion and ask what you think. Don't resist his leadership (except on moral issues, such as having a sexual encounter very early on in your relationship). This can give him the impression that you don't respect him. Refusing to follow him will make him feel like you are denying his masculinity, which is a huge mistake.

Even if he makes mistakes or things turn out to be a disaster, you will need to keep your opinions to yourself and try to find the bright side of the situation. I should also mention that women have a way of showing disapproval without saying a word. Therefore, make sure that your facial expressions and body language don't show signs of disappointment. A man can easily pick up on your disapproval based on your actions. If you don't trust that he will be able to make decisions and lead you in a way that you feel is satisfactory, that means you really don't trust his judgment and he's most likely not the right man for you.

Also, it's important to remember to not be overly competitive with your man. Being feminine is about being cooperative, not trying to compete. Most guys do not enjoy coming home to a woman that is trying to upstage him and rub her victories in his face. Save the competitiveness for things that aren't taken seriously like board games and play fights.

Don't misunderstand me, I am not telling you that you need to be a weak little woman that stays at home and doesn't have her own career or ambitions. It's actually quite the opposite because even if you make the most money in the relationship, a secure man won't have a problem with that. Just don't ever throw that in your man's face, especially during an argument. In fact, your higher income should never be used to leverage control over the spending in the household or in your relationship.

Remember that you don't need to have the overly feminine side of your personality on display at all times. Most men have relationships with women who tend to have masculine qualities as well, especially when playing sports or in a work environment. Just don't forget to pull out your feminine side when you're alone together. In other words, don't bring your aggressive work attitude home with you.

In your everyday decisions don't get in the habit of taking the lead on tasks that men are usually in charge of. He won't appreciate you telling him what to do and how to do it. However, it's okay for you to take initiative in well-established activities. More specifically, I am referring to things like what to make for dinner, if you are the one that cooks of course.

It's easy to attract a man by being feminine, which really means allowing him to feel comfortable with you because you show him that you respect his opinions and trust his judgment. Make him feel appreciated by showing him love and care along with your natural beauty. This will bring joy to his life and make him feel nurtured as well. In return, he will want to do whatever he can to please you too.

When your man feels this way, you won't

have to worry about him leaving you for another woman. He will have no desire to lose the special feelings that the two of you share. Even if some other women may be more attractive physically, they don't possess the inner qualities that he enjoys with you.

Chapter Six

Intelligence

Another quality that men want in a woman is intelligence. We've all heard the stereotypes of men being love struck by the gorgeous blonde without a brain in her head. This goes hand in hand with the idea that a man can't handle a woman who is his intellectual equal. It's a fairly common belief that men are intimidated by women who are intelligent. Because of the different ways that men and women are hard wired so to speak, this is true to a point, but there's a lot more to it. Men do want intelligent women that know how to show it without putting them down as men.

The Dumb Blonde Stereotype

Yes, men are attracted to any woman who has great looks, regardless of her hair color, but intelligence level has little to do with initial physical attraction. The attraction is purely physical and he most likely just wants to have sex with her and is not thinking much beyond that. In these circumstances he isn't thinking about marrying her and starting a family. It's when a man gets to know a woman that her intelligence level could be what ends up making or breaking the relationship.

Forget The Stereotypes And Get The Real Story

When stereotypes are taken as the truth, they cause people to believe things that have a little bit of truth but miss the mark when you try to apply them to everyone. There is actually a smaller number of men who just want a gorgeous woman with a great body to meet their needs. It goes far beyond that when a man is looking for a serious relationship that could become long term. Men want intelligent women who don't put them down or try to upstage them. Everyone wants to be able to feel good about themselves and men are no exception.

How To Make Yourself Appear More Intelligent To Men Without Upstaging Or Emasculating Them

The cardinal rule here is to think about how you would feel if a man took aspects of your feminine role and showed you he was much better at them. If he could sew, keep a house and was a better cook than you it may sting a little. Upstaging a man by talking over his head on a topic you know, or by correcting a mistake he makes in front of others can make him feel really lousy. Your intelligence is something that can be used naturally but not flaunted so as to hurt his pride in being masculine. There are just some things that have to be understood and agreed upon. This is one of them. If you protect his masculine pride he will appreciate and respect you more for it. The odds are that he returns the favor for you by not bragging about all of the things he is good at. It becomes a kind of mutual respect.

Don't Throw Out The Baby With The Bath Water And Hide Your Intelligence

From Men

Acting less intelligent than you really are is really a form of dishonesty. It can be insulting to him if he knows it's an act and it's kind of condescending. It may end up doing more harm than good in the long run. By just being yourself and being considerate of his feelings as a man you will do just fine. It's not really that complicated once you know how it works.

Intelligence is an attractive quality to men looking for an equal partner. Making the right connections is what dating is all about. Searching for a compatible partner involves knowing a person for who they truly are and either accepting them, or walking away. Intelligent women are most apt to attract a man who is looking for a stable partner. While a beautiful woman may attract most men on a sexual level regardless of their IQ, if they are not a good match in other important areas, such as intellect, there might not be enough that they have in common to keep them together.

Intelligent Women Have A Lot To Offer Men

The truth of the matter is that quality men who are looking for a long-term relationship will be attracted to a woman whose attitudes, values and ability to reason are close to their own. The reason for this is that apart from sexual attraction, couples need to be able to communicate with each other. If you can't sit down and have an enjoyable conversation with each other, it's like speaking different languages. Men enjoy being able to talk about things that matter to them with their partners. If he believes she won't understand what he's talking about, he may just keep quiet instead of having a productive two way conversation. One sure way to tell that a man is comfortable with your intelligence is when he asks your advice on important decisions. This shows he values your opinion and feels no threat.

Intelligent women are easier to relate to and there is less chance of misunderstandings happening. A woman with the ability to reason and make sound choices will make a better partner because she will be more of a help than a hindrance. She will be able to help manage personal finance and other business without the need for constant help from him. This takes a major load off of men as they do not have to take full responsibility for paying bills, troubleshooting problems with the home or making decisions because of a partner who depends on him to handle it all.

Intelligence well done is a quality in women that men value. Men who have fantastic physical attributes often get more attention than some women. This can make a woman feel jealous or like her role as a woman is being threatened in some way. This is the type of reaction that a decent and well-intentioned man may have to encounter from a woman, but it doesn't have to become a problem if it's handled in the right way. A woman can help pull this off without acting like she is less intelligent. Flaunting what you know, showboating and upstaging others are some of the biggest turnoffs for men. You can take a far better approach by understanding the differences in feminine and masculine psyche when it comes to these matters.

In short, you like to have your feminine pride and he likes to have his masculine pride. By understanding these things you will most likely find that a man will appreciate your intelligence and enjoy the time you spend together. When you use your intelligence in the right ways, it will be powerfully attractive to men.

Chapter Seven

Innocence

Men place an extremely high value on purity and innocence in women. This is especially true when a man is interested in a serious relationship that could include marriage and starting a family. How to exactly define purity and innocence can be a little tricky because everyone has their own set of values and morals that determine what that means to them. Each man has his own beliefs in this area and it depends on a lot of different things like his upbringing while growing up, his past experiences and what he has learned from what he has seen through life. He may view purity and innocence in terms whether or not she is a virgin, the number of sexual partners she has had or he might define it as her personal commitment to a single partner in a relationship.

Even though differences in values help shape these opinions in men, most generally, women who are or have been involved in the sex industry like porn stars, call girls or strippers are not considered by most men to be either pure or innocent. While men may enjoy their company in the short term, they aren't usually the first choice for marriage.

You may be thinking that it's a double standard for men to believe it's okay for them to enjoy a diverse sexual life and then prefer a woman who hasn't. Fair or not, this is how it is. Blame society for this one. It doesn't mean that he will continue to do this after he commits to you. Because of the hoopla made about the way men are attracted to beautiful women that are easy to get into bed, women who are the opposites of the glam queens who put out may feel like they are plain or boring and without the sex appeal of their more experienced counterparts. When it comes to serious matters of the heart, this couldn't be further from the truth.

Reasons Why Men Prefer Purity And Innocence In Women

Men are looking for a genuine loving relationship with all of the bells and whistles. They know that a one night stand with a woman that gives it away freely won't give them the security of a faithful and loving partner that they can come home to every night. One night stands amount to nothing more than a sexual encounter and physical release. There is no expectation of a beneficial or lasting bond being formed. It's more like a recreational activity versus a lifestyle. Men usually only do this when they can't get the love and affection of a real woman who is innocent and pure. It's merely a substitute for what they really desire.

Theory On Why Men Prefer Pure And Innocent Women

It makes sense to a man that a woman's track record can signal how she will act when she is with him. If she has had sex without commitment in the past, marriage may not prevent her from repeating it. A lack of purity can mean that he can't trust her. Innocent women who have kept themselves pure are easier to trust and less likely to cheat.

Women who dress in sexually provocative ways or flirt with other men to gain their attention make it difficult for men to trust them. If she is initiating this behavior, it's similar to running an advertisement and increases the chances of a sexual encounter.

A woman who cheats has the advantage of selecting a man with better genes to improve the quality of her offspring. Tricking her husband into thinking it's his child gives her the additional advantage of having him use his resources to raise the child. This is one of the reasons why men prefer pure and innocent women for marriage or serious relationships.

If a woman becomes pregnant the man wants to be able to trust that the child is his without wondering. No man desires to raise another man's child under the false pretense that it's his. It uses up his resources without the benefits of adding his genetic code to the gene pool.

This theory talks about humans at the

biological level and our natural urge to produce as many children as possible. At this level, women are more concerned with the quality of the children they produce while men are concerned with the quantity because men are able to produce far more children than women.

This is only an explanation of the theory that relates to our primitive animal instincts. It's the part of biological nature that ensures that our species continues to exist. Through social conditioning and the development of moral consciences, our behaviors are much more refined than this or the world would be total chaos. Aside from the theory, it is still true that men prefer to be with a wholesome woman over others who lack purity and innocence.

How To Show Your Innocence And Purity To Men

The way you dress is the first place to start. If your clothing is sexually provocative it sends the signal that you're advertising sexual availability to men. More modest apparel that you would be comfortable in around anyone, including your grandmother or his parents is a sign of purity. The next important thing to do is to mind the way that you behave. Being flirtatious with other men, using crude or coarse language do not show innocence or purity. If your language and actions are more uplifting and positive, avoiding negative attitudes that are seen in some women who have been around the block, you're sending out all the right signals. Lastly, smoking, excessive drinking, using drugs, gambling and any other obsessive behaviors are traits that are associated with a lack of innocence. These are just a few tips to help you get the gist of how men perceive women who are pure and innocent versus those who are not.

When men choose a life partner, they want someone that they can trust and depend on to be there. This is someone that he can share intimacy with and build a life and family with by working together to reach their dreams. This is the type of woman that gives him the things that he really needs and values in a partner. On the other hand, women who lack purity are more likely to sleep with other men and to be untrustworthy in other areas of life as well. Men know that there would be mistrust and doubt in the relationship. With purity and innocence, he won't have to wonder about what his wife is doing when he's not around. He will know that his heart and well-being are safe in her hands.

Chapter Eight

Presence

Most women have the ability to do several things at one time without missing a beat. Their ability to multitask is amazing. Think about how many times you, or the women you know listen to music or watch a video while working out, or talk on the phone and do housework while applying makeup at the same time. It's fairly rare to see a woman doing just one single thing at a time. Although this is an amazing talent, it isn't one that is appealing to men. When a man sees you whizzing around like a Tasmanian devil, they get the impression that your energies and focus are going in too many directions. Truthfully, men are more attracted to women who can focus on just one single thing at a time.

Why Multitasking Is Unattractive To Men

When you are in a flurry doing two or three things at a time, you send off certain vibes. This is because multitasking is a lot like the mental thought processes that take place in our minds. Stream of thought consciousness moves quickly from one thought to another and spiderwebs even further from there.

There are many men and women who have thoughts, when interacting with others, that are jumping around and making them feel as though people do not like them or accept them for who they are. They are reminded of their faults as their thoughts move around different topics, including all the work they still have left to do. There are also streams of thought that make them critical and judgmental of others because of the negativity they are feeling from earlier streams. In other words, our thoughts often keep us from paying full attention to the people we interact with.

Interacting with a person who flings themselves in many directions at once gives the impression that they have something to prove to others. This is a sign that they feel inadequate within themselves, or maybe even have some agenda. They also have a nervousness about them that is easy to detect. They often think the worst of others because their thoughts tend to go in so many directions. Nervous energy of this type usually generates negative thoughts.

These vibes don't make anyone feel great, in fact, they repel most of us and they are definitely not the thing that will attract men to women who have this going on. You may have seen this happen in your own experience. If you are a woman who tends to multitask and a guy shows interest in you and then becomes nervous or uncomfortable, he could be catching negative vibes from your mental activity. Believe me, thoughts send out energy that other people can feel. They connect us to some past experiences big time.

Women Who Seem Distracted Are Less Appealing To Men

Too much activity, whether it's mental or

physical, shows that a woman is distracted and not focused upon the person she is interacting with. Imagine that you are trying to get to know a person, and you can tell his mind is going a mile a minute. You don't know what his thoughts are about, but you can tell as he speaks with you he's there for a minute, then in his mind, he is somewhere else. Would this make you want to continue the conversation? It sends the message that you are scattered and may not be reliable or dependable. This is one of the reasons why men tend to avoid women who have a lack of single focus. It's nice to be able to sit down and focus on each other when you're trying to become better acquainted.

What Is Presence In Women?

Presence is the ability to be present in the moment. When you are present, you are not only physically there, but your thoughts and focus is placed upon a single thing or person at a time. Your mind doesn't wander aimlessly and take you away to random places. Men can sense when a woman has presence by her demeanor. When she is present, she is more relaxed and more focused upon what is happening at that moment in time. She is easier to talk to and is much less distracted than someone who is checking off a mental list or building a scenario in her head. She may have fleeting thoughts, e.g., "I like him, " "I wonder if he likes me" and so on, but the thoughts are directly related to what is going on at the time. This sends the message that she is emotionally available to him. If she is easily distracted, it's much like closing the door in his face.

Why Men Want To See Presence In Women

Plain and simple, men want your undivided attention. If you seem distracted the majority of the time, he senses it and takes it as a sign that there are more important things on your mind. Pursuing a relationship with you may be futile because you are unable or unwilling to give him what he wants and needs from you. There is a big difference between just listening to the words of the person who is speaking to you, and being engaged in the interaction. When you are engaged, you are fully focused upon your interactions, and committing your thought processes to the person you are with. Without presence in a woman, there isn't a lot there to make a man want to interact with her again.

Presence Is Required For Falling In Love

When you fall in love, you want to spend time with that special person. Time spent together goes by more quickly as you are totally absorbed in each other. The moments when you are not speaking, you are quietly contemplating one another. Nothing ruins this beautiful process quicker than distractions. How can you fall in love with a man if you cannot focus upon him?

Men who are falling in love with a woman may feel a sense of rejection and feeling disrespected if she has a tendency to mentally drift to other places, particularly as their new bond is forming. Any man who has been disappointed by this in the past will be particularly alert for the signs, and avoid women that are likely to be this way. If you want to attract a man and keep his interest, you must show him that you have presence.

Selective Presence Creates Problems

Men are aware of how you interact with other people. If you only give your full attention to people who have something to offer you, he may think that you are just out for what you can get from people, or that you are needy. This is because women who feel content in themselves and have all of their needs met have more energy and are less distracted. They aren't constantly plotting and planning mentally. They tend to give freely to others. Be careful about faking presence because you're apt to slip up and get caught in your distractions. This will only make you appear to be an opportunistic person, which is a turn off for men.

How To Become Fully Present

Being fully present the majority of the time is a good habit to start. It may take some work, but most things that are worthwhile do. Here are a few great tips that will get you on your way. First, know who you are. If you are a confident woman you will have high self-esteem, which means that you like and accept yourself for who you are. Believe that you are worthwhile and embrace all of the positive aspects of the self. By doing this, you eliminate neediness and the distracting thoughts that go with it. Negative thoughts and mental distractions are generally caused by feeling bad about yourself in some way.

When you have inner contentment and are at peace with who you are, there is no need for the turmoil and it occupies less of your thinking. Your focus will become much sharper when you get the mental clutter out of the way. Worries about being accepted by others, feeling inadequate, and your criticism of others tend to fall by the wayside. You'll find that you will be able to more naturally focus on others because there are no other distractions. This will not only make you more attractive to quality men, but it will also help you in all of the relationships in your life.

Getting rid of this type of emotional baggage is similar to cleaning clutter out of your home. Becoming more organized physically will also help you to drop some of the emotional chaos. Keep your surroundings neat and organized so they won't be a mental distraction. You are doing a metaphoric house cleaning inside. Plus, taking care of the things you see with your eyes will be a good inspiration. Take care of any business matters that need attending. In order to stay organized and focused, take care of commitments that are left hanging, as they can become distractions.

Finally, make a pact with yourself to place limits on the amount of multitasking you do. This is a good mental practice that will actually help to improve your focus because you will be honing this important skill. In fact, studies have shown that multitasking actually slows you down and makes you much less productive. This is because your brain needs time to shift gears and reach an optimal speed every time you jump from one task to another.

By following these tips, you'll begin to notice positive changes in yourself. These are changes that will make you feel better about yourself, and in turn, give you the ability to be present in whatever moment you are in.

As you can see, men highly value presence in a woman. It tells them that she is able to focus upon them and provide her undivided attention. They know that they won't be taking a back seat to her chore list or the internal mental chatter of her self-doubts. Men are more strongly attracted to women who tend to focus upon a single thing at a time because it signals that they are emotionally available. Women who come across as being distracted by trying to do too many things at once give the impression that they will never be able to devote their full attention to a man. This means he will not be able to gain the satisfaction of getting his needs met by her. If you want to be more attractive to a man, then you must be present on a consistent basis.

Chapter Nine

Youthfulness

All women know that the appearance of youthfulness is a quality that is attractive to men. There are reasons for this that are rooted deep in our natural instincts. This has to do with the drive and nature of mankind to continue the species. While this may sound a bit unfair to older women, it's simply the fact of the matter. Younger women in their 20s and 30s are prime for child bearing. This is just part of nature's way of ensuring that the population continues, and men are driven by these natural urges and desires to be attracted to women who show signs that they are capable of reproducing.

This doesn't necessarily mean that men will not be attracted to older women, it just means that the prompting of nature makes them prone to be more attracted to younger women. There are men who may not consciously want to have children for various reasons and so this drive happens at a much deeper level. This is the drive to have sex with women who appear fertile. The good news is that it isn't a woman's actual age in years that matters, it's how youthful she appears to a man.

How To Appear More Youthful

If you are a woman who is past the ideal child bearing age you have a lot of different options at your disposal for appearing more youthful. First of all, take care of your health. By eating sensibly, keeping off excess pounds and staying fit, your body will be more toned and attractive. Staying well hydrated and taking measures to protect your skin from premature aging will also make you look younger. In addition to this, avoiding the over use of alcohol, tobacco, caffeine and other unhealthy habits will make a difference in how you look overall. One of the most important factors in maintaining good health and a youthful appearance is to get plenty of rest and not let stress bog you down. When you're exhausted or under a lot of pressure, it can cause you to appear older.

Men Are Attracted To Women With Longer Hair

From a man's perspective, the way you style your hair will also affect their perception of your youthfulness. Most men prefer long hair in women because as women age, they usually begin moving towards shorter and shorter styles. Men associate longer hair with youthfulness. Hair that is at least shoulder length is recommended because men do find this attractive in women. As I said earlier, long hair doesn't suit every woman; therefore, you should use your best judgment to determine which hairstyle makes you appear more youthful.

The Way You Dress Can Make You Appear More Youthful

The style of clothing that you wear will also affect a man's estimation of your youthfulness. You can still tastefully wear clothing types that younger women are wearing. Choose styles that flatter your figure but don't make you look like a hip granny. You'll be able to find something in the middle that works. If you have a nice figure, jeans that accentuate your curves are always a good choice. It's important to choose your clothing style very carefully because it's easy to get stuck in a rut wearing outfits that make you look like you are much older than you are. Don't let fear of the opinions of other women your age and older stop you from dressing in more youthful styles. If it looks classy on you and it's in good taste, go for it.

Accentuate Your Best Assets

The way you apply your makeup can also affect the youthfulness of your appearance. For example, some products will help you hide dark circles under the eyes or soften age lines that have formed. So long as they are natural and healthy for your skin, these are some great ways to take a few years off of your face. A great foundation can help to give your skin an even tone and healthy glow that most younger women have. Be careful with cosmetics though. If applied correctly, they can make you look younger, but if not, they can actually make you look older. It's best to go for a sheer and natural look when using cosmetics. Take good care of your hands and feet, and keep them well manicured and looking their best. The small details can count.

A Youthful Attitude And Outlook On Life Is Attractive To Men

When you remain youthful inside, it shows on the outside. Life is full of its ups and downs and just the stress of life experiences can make a woman start to show signs of aging. Frown lines deepen and form unattractive wrinkling, and also, a negative attitude can cause you to look older because of facial expressions you can develop.

When your emotions are negative it shows on your face and in your posture. Having a more relaxed and carefree attitude reduces the formation of lines, but it does something even more powerful and attractive to men. It allows you to keep a sparkle in your eyes, and to have the vigor and excitement towards life that younger women have. If you have a youthful spirit, it will show in your appearance, your approach to life, and the energy that you send out to others. Men are keen on picking up on these subtleties.

Hopefully now you have a better understanding of why men are attracted to women who appear more youthful. It is nature in action more than a conscious choice. Women who are past the ideal age for childbearing can still make themselves attractive to men by making themselves appear to be more youthful. Women who take care of their physical bodies and their emotional health will appear more youthful. By avoiding behaviors that lead to premature aging of the skin and body, it's easier to maintain a younger appearance naturally, for longer.

Women who have a youthful spirit will not only appear younger, but their behaviors will send the message of youthfulness to men. It will show in their physical appearance, their attitudes, behaviors, and the energy that men feel when they are around them.

By paying attention to important details like hairstyles, clothing, and the proper use of cosmetics, women can improve their looks by adopting the trends that younger women are following. Actual age in years is not always the

factor that men consider, but it is the appearance
of youthfulness in women that attracts them the
most.

Chapter Ten

Strength

Strength is a quality in women that men value highly, even though it's not a trait that is commonly associated with women, or with the list of things that are attractive to men. The norm is that strength is associated with being masculine and weakness, to a point, associated with the feminine gender. The reason for this is quite simple. Men are generally physically stronger than women, and historically, women have served more submissive roles as the weaker sex. Some may argue this point, but it's still a fact that influences the way the majority of people think. But strength comes in many different forms. It's more than being able to toss a caber in the Scotland games or change a tire on a car. Inner strength is the powerful quality that we are talking about here.

What Is Inner Strength In A Woman?

Inner strength is a woman's ability to use wisdom and make intelligent decisions. Her ability to handle adversity when it comes, and come out on top shows her inner strength. Women with this kind of strength are confident, emotionally stable, and competent in the areas they need to be. A strong woman will not back away from a challenge, but will meet it head on and figure out the best course of action while she's moving towards it. She's able to think on her feet and keep peace and order in her home.

Is Submission A Weakness?

Women who allow men to take the lead in a relationship are not necessarily weak because they choose a subordinate role. This is a matter of preference. It takes a lot of hard work to help a partner in a supportive role. There is a lot of work that takes place behind the scenes that often requires a heck of a lot of time and energy.

Being an emotional support is something that is hard to place a value on as it allows the man to move more confidently forward in completing his responsibilities. There is nothing wrong with a man assuming a masculine role while a woman performs the tasks associated with the feminine. Men appreciate this show of confidence in their abilities to lead and it strengthens the appreciation and respect he feels for a woman. Strength in these areas serves as a strong source of attraction for men.

Why Men Are Attracted To Strength In Women

When men see strength in women they are more likely to believe that she is competent and capable of handling anything that life may throw at them as a couple. She is not likely to back away from problems and leave him holding the bag. She is more apt to be in the relationship for the long haul. This gives men a tremendous feeling of security and safety.

Why Weakness In Women Is Not Attractive To Men

Women who convey inner weakness to men

are sending the impression that they are incapable of pulling their weight and will probably end up being a burden. Weak women tend to flounder in making daily decisions, and when trouble hits, they fold up like a house of cards. Men realize that they may not be able to rely on them to be an equal partner and help to build a life together. What man would want to spend the rest of his life taking care of the needs and wants of another adult that cannot do the same for him? This is one of the reasons why men are attracted to strength in women.

Men see women who are weak as potential users that will only value them for what they can get them to do for them. Most men are happy to provide for the needs of their women who are pulling their share in different ways. It's a two way street. Just as women don't want to be used by men for sex and keeping their laundry and meals served, a man doesn't want to be used as an object for support, hard work and compensated at her convenience. He is looking for a partner that will give and take alongside of him. With this in mind, it's easy to see why men value strength in women.

How To Present Yourself As A Strong

Woman

High-quality men have become experts at spotting weakness in women as a survival skill. If he is going to be attracted to you, avoiding a show of weakness is vital, as is showing him your inner strength. He needs to see certain qualities in you that include strength of character, intelligence, competence, confidence, self-control, emotional maturity and independence. This is not the time to play the part of a weak and helpless female.

Intelligence is shown in your ability to be socially adept, to have gained knowledge over a wide variety of topics through life experience, to be able to express your creativity and to possess good articulation skills in conversation.

Emotional maturity means that you are not prone to outbursts, mood swings, unreasonable fears or unpredictable behaviors that can seem out of place. Blowing up on someone and venting is a sign that you're not in control. You want to project a firm even control over your emotions that shows your stability and self-confidence.

Confidence and competence are shown when

you believe in your abilities and actually know what you're doing. You're able to get the job done right the first time. These are both tremendous strengths that men value.

Independence is one of the most important strengths that a woman can possess. It means that you are able to take care of yourself and in a partnership you are ready, willing and able to pull your share at a minimum. By showing a man your independence, you are letting him see that you are not needy and you don't require him to provide for your every need and wish. You're also sending the message that you would make a good partner. But this must be balanced. While it's always a good idea to offer to pull your weight, don't insist if he declines. Let him do the things he wants to do for you without argument. This makes him feel good about himself.

Strength of character is seen in people who know what they want, go after it and put in the hard work to make it happen. It's refusing to give up when the going gets tough. You maintain your integrity, grit your teeth if needed and keep going until the job is done. Men find this to be of incredible value in women because it's a sign that she won't walk away when life has its rough spots. She is more apt to work harder as a partner to get through to the other side.

Men know that strength in women is a quality that is to be treasured, and this is why it is a powerful source of attraction for them. Men who are looking for a long-term serious relationship with a woman area the most attracted by her strengths that tell him she will be as dedicated as he. He has less reason to wonder if she will take advantage of him or use him, but rather, he is encouraged that she will provide as much support and affection for him as he does for her.

Conclusion

If you read the introduction you may remember that I promised to reveal the underlying factor or the foundation for all ten qualities that you read about in this book. Well, I will do that in a few minutes, but first I want us to quickly review all the important things that I want you to take away from this book and apply to your dating life. As we do this, you may want to try to determine what this one big characteristic is, if you haven't done so already.

- Physical appearance is not as important as your inner qualities, despite what the media and today's society has to say about it. All you truly need is a pleasing physical appearance. Exercise regularly and eat healthy in order to stay fit and look your best. Grow your hair to shoulder length unless it doesn't suit you. Wear clothes that accentuate your physique without making you look trashy. Remember that less is more when it comes to cosmetics. You have done your job as long as you have tried to look your best and feel comfortable with the way you look. What others think doesn't matter at this point.

- It's crucial to radiate high self-esteem in order to attract quality men. Self-esteem is all about liking, accepting and respecting yourself. Well-adjusted men are very good at discerning women with high self-esteem from those who lack it. Men find that low self-esteem tends to bring unwanted drama into their lives. In order to start building your self-esteem you must begin to like, love and accept yourself for who you are, even as you try to improve yourself in the process. This means that you must never blame yourself for anything that you have done or will do. Instead, you should simply accept it, acknowledge it and make an effort to change.

- Confidence is a set of beliefs that make you trust and even expect that everything will turn out well despite many challenges that may be in your way. This is something that quality men find extremely attractive in women. Confidence and self-esteem is a two way street because one helps strengthen the other. Your confidence will project a successful image to a man, which in turn will make him think that being in a relationship with you will add value to his life in a positive way. Building your confidence has a lot to do with building your self-esteem because when you value yourself you also develop a positive attitude towards life, which in turn will help you trust your abilities. Remember that confidence is developed primarily when you challenge and apply yourself despite being scared to do something new.

- Most men love femininity in women and wouldn't be able to have a fulfilling life without one. Don't misinterpret the true meaning of femininity though. Being a female doesn't necessarily make you feminine. Being feminine is all about the energy that you project from inside. In order to attract men you must be comfortable with being feminine in front of them. This means that you must not resist his leadership. If he wants to help you with something, let him help. In fact, men love it when a woman asks him for help once in a while because it makes him feel valued as a man. In other words, when you operate with your feminine energy it allows men to operate with their masculine energy, which is vital for a healthy relationship.

- Quality men always look for women who emit positive emotions. Men want to be around a woman who is happy more often than not and who smiles frequently. When a woman is fun to be around, it makes men feel at ease and happy too. On the other hand, men typically despise women who are always unhappy, bored, moody, demanding and angry, which makes sense because who likes to be around energy vampires? Remember that you want men to think that you are easy to please and not the other way around.

From a man's perspective, if you are full of positive emotions and a joy to be around, it indicates that you are not high maintenance. A positive personality will make you look a lot more approachable and attractive.

- Intelligence makes a woman very desirable to men for quite a few reasons. One of them being that men view intelligence as a huge asset to the relationship as long as she uses it in a way that doesn't upstage or emasculate them. A quality man will never fall in love with you no matter how beautiful you look unless you can show him that you have a beautiful mind as well. In order to be perceived as intelligent by a man, you must possess creativity and knowledge. But more importantly, you must be able to articulate yourself efficiently. Don't get me wrong, you don't need to be a genius in order to appear intelligent. All you have to do is display a desire to learn, grow and communicate efficiently.

- Regardless of whether it's fair or not, men prefer to have serious relationships with women who they considered to be innocent and pure. In other words, men don't generally look to marry women that they would find in a bar or a club. These women are more often looked at as someone to have fun with rather than a serious candidate for a relationship. Remember that it's the way you dress, talk, and even think that conveys your purity and innocence to a man. Something to also keep in mind is that habits like smoking, drinking and taking drugs are definitely a big turn off for high-quality men.

- Another major characteristic that men want to see in you is the ability to stay present when communicating with them. If they see that your mind is constantly jumping from one thought to another with no relation to what you are talking about, then this will definitely hinder you chances of appearing attractive in his eyes. Men want to see your full and undivided attention. I should also mention that you can't just display total presence when communicating with the guy that you are interested in and then use your presence selectively when communicating with other people. This is because you don't want to give him the impression that you are one of those people who only pay attention when you need something from someone. Becoming fully present is a skill and it will take some practice, but it's absolutely doable and developing your self-esteem and confidence is a great place to start.

- Youthfulness is another quality that men prefer in women because it's something that was biologically embedded in our psyche. The good news is that you don't have to actually be in your 20s (when you are most fertile), you just need to possess a youthful appearance that men find naturally attractive. The best way to appear more youthful is by taking care of your body, which means eating properly and exercising regularly. You also want to make sure that your hair, skin and clothes all work to make you look younger. In many ways, a youthful appearance also stems from your spirit and outlook on life. It's a good idea to find a life purpose and strive every day to fulfill it. When combined, all these things will help you seem and feel younger, and therefore attract like-minded men.

- Strength is another quality that a man desires in a woman that he wants to establish a relationship with. What we are talking about here is not physical strength but rather strength of character. This type of strength encapsulates confidence, competence, self-control and emotional stability. In other words, strength gives you the ability to be independent when required. A quality man doesn't want to be in a relationship with a woman who is needy and can't take care of herself. What he does want is a woman who is willing to love and accept him for who he is instead of how much money he makes and what he can do for her. Once he sees that she loves, supports and appreciates him for who he is he will undoubtedly do the same for her.

Now that we have reviewed all ten qualities that a man wants in a woman, were you able to figure out what the foundation is for all of those qualities?

As they say, the biggest things are usually hidden in plain sight. So if you answered self-esteem, self-confidence, dignity or self-respect, then you are correct. All of those fit under one category, but it's not the category that matters, it's what they all collectively mean that does. If you take a look at all the qualities that we have covered in this book then you will notice that practically all of them hinge on how you feel about yourself and your abilities in relation to the outside world and society at large.

Why is this so important, you ask? Well, it's because individuals who are abundant in this many ways will experience a completely different and more fulfilling life than those who are on the opposite end of the spectrum. Putting it simply, high self-confidence, self-esteem, self-respect or dignity, regardless of what you call it, will significantly improve your quality of life. This applies to your dating life as well. There is a universal law that states, "As within, so without." When your thoughts and outlooks change, so will the way other people see you, think about you and treat you.

www.ingramcontent.com/pod-product-compliance
Lightning Source LLC
Chambersburg PA
CBHW060153290526
45789CB00003B/1020